The land
of religions

Vincenzo Berghella

Copyright Page

Copyright year: 2011

Copyright notice: by Vincenzo Berghella

All rights reserved

ISBN No: 978-0-578-14430-6

From the same author:

- **Obstetric Evidence Based Guidelines.** Informa Healthcare, London, UK, and New York, USA (2007) [English]
- **Maternal Fetal Evidence Based Guidelines.** Informa Healthcare, London, UK, and New York, USA (2007) [English]
- **Laughter, the best medicine. Jokes for everyone.** (2007) [English]
- **Ridere, la migliore medicina. Barzellette per bambini.** (2007) [Italiano]
- **My favorite quotes.** (2009) [English]
- **In medio stat virtus – Citazioni d'autore.** (2009) [Italiano]
- **Quello che di voi vive in me.** (2009) [Italiano]
- **Dall'altra parte dell'oceano.** (2010) [Italiano] [Translated in: **On the other side of the ocean.** (2013) [English]
- **Preterm Birth: Prevention and Management.** Wiley-Blackwell. Oxford, United Kingdom. (2010) [English]
- **From father to son.** (2010) [English]
- **Sollazzi.** (2010) [Italiano]

- **The land of religions.** (2011) [English] [Translated in: **La terra delle religioni.** (2013) [Italiano]
- **Giramondo.** (2011) [Italiano]
- **Obstetric Evidence Based Guidelines.** Informa Healthcare, London, UK, and New York, USA (2012; Second Edition) [English]
- **Maternal Fetal Evidence Based Guidelines.** Informa Healthcare, London, UK, and New York, USA (2012; Second Edition)[English]
- **Trip to London.** (2012) [English]
- **Il primo amore non si scorda mai.** (2012) [Italiano]
- **Maldives.** (2013) [English]
- **Russia.** (2013) [English]
- **Happiness. The scientific path to achieving well-being.** (2014) [English]

To those who are tolerant, and enjoy history and travel

Introduction

In November 2010 I've visited Israel for the first time in my life. These are my recollections of an unforgettable trip, to an exceptional place.

I truly hope you enjoy this story.

Vincenzo

Tuesday, November 23, 2010

As you walk to the gate of your international flight, your trip begins. You look around, and see people wearing different clothes, speaking foreign languages. Today we see men wearing only black. Black jacket, black pants, black shoes. And black hat, with a wide rim. And a beard. Some other men are wearing a head cover. Their beard is much shorter. Most wear glasses. Women are wearing conservative dresses, showing no knees, not even ankles, certainly no shoulders or elbows.

We are going to Tel Aviv, a non-stop flight from Philadelphia. In 12 hours we'll be in another continent. While I've traveled already to 5 different continents, going to Israel for the first time is very exciting. I have been preparing this trip in detail for about a year. We kept Elisheva at the travel agency in Tel Aviv very busy, and we have changed details of the trip at least 4 times, to get the most for time and money. I have a detailed word document of what will happen every day.

I've been studying for months, as I love to do before any big trip. I've read *Exodus*, the wonderful fiction/non-fiction account of the War of liberation, by Leon Uris. I've read the Fodor's guide for Israel. I've read in Italian the history of the Jewish people (*My people*), by Abba Eban. Last year, in 2009, I've visited Berlin and the nearby concentration camp. Also in 2009, I was at the Holocaust Memorial Museum in Washington.

I've dated Betsy, a pretty and bright Jewish girl, for over a year, from 1989 to 1990. I could have married her, but we were probably too young. I've attended the Jewish wedding of her brother, in Cincinnati, and saw them break the glass. I helped carry the chairs in which they sat and were celebrated.

My last name, Berghella, apparently derives from Van den Berg. My father states that our ancestor came from northern Europe, and was most probably Jewish. My religion, Christianity, was founded by a Jewish prophet, Jesus Christ. In many different ways, since adulthood, I've felt a little bit of Judaism in me, and I've been fascinated by its history. I have never had a problem with Jewish people, and I've in fact admired them. Most of my bosses have been Jewish, including Dr. Zinberg in New York, and Drs. Wapner and Weinstein in Philadelphia. Some of the smartest doctor colleagues I know are Jewish. They are dedicated, hard working, fair. I've always admired their commitment. The ones I've seen in leadership or prominent positions have deserved them.

Their history is unique. Religions usually cross different countries. Islam covers much of North Africa, the Middle East, and has Indonesia as the country with most Muslims. Christianity is everywhere, Europe, Africa, South and Central America in particular. Buddhism is common in much of Asia. Hinduism is mostly in India.

Until 1948, Judaism had no country in particular. It was spread a bit all over, after the Diaspora. No other religion has suffered as much. I believe most wars have had some religious reasons. Judaism has just been fought against for millennia. Perhaps because, of all current well-known religions, it is the oldest.

You feel in a ghetto from the get-go. We are obliged to go to a second tight security point, the only passengers in the whole airport to have to do so. Now the percentage of Israelis is well over the majority. There are 2 lines. A older man, perhaps 60 years old, chooses the right one. My son Andrea moves to the left. As the right line is stuck and slow, the older Jew wants now to step on the left line, in front of Andrea, unaware. The Israeli man, with a sarcastic smile, gets a bit mad at Andrea. He tells us, Paola and me: "He should learn manners." We apologize to him, and reassure Andrea it was the older man who 'cut' the line. I understand better now what being a 'sabra' means. This is a fruit that has prickles on the outside, but is sweet on the inside. Native-born Israeli are known as 'sabras.' I've read that Israelis, from millennia of persecution, are a bit tough, pushy. We get a taste of it even at the Tel Aviv gate in Philly.

Israel was founded in 1948, after 2 millennia of Diaspora. But the history of the Jewish people is much older.

Circa **1800 BC**, **Abraham** marks the beginning of the Patriarcal age, and is the first 'Jew' in history. He came from Ur of the Chaldees, in ancient Persia. Funny to think that now Iraq is one of Israel's worse enemies, as the origin of the Jews is from that land. God promised Abraham that his descendants would inherit the land of Canaan. This is currently Israel, and before Israel it was called Palestine by the British between 1917 and 1948. So Abraham descended into the land of Canaan. Abraham did not have descendants until late in age. His wife **Sarah** gave birth to Isaac when very old, 90 years old! As a high-risk obstetrician, I know this is an exaggeration. In fact, the word 'yitzhak' comes from 'to laugh' in Hebrew. God asks Abraham to sacrifice Isaac, which Abraham prepares to do. But at last God retreats his wish.

Isaac, Abraham's son, and the second of the three Patriarchs, married **Rebekah** (second Matriarch). Rebekah is the daughter of Abraham's brother. Isaac and Rebekah are therefore paternal first cousins, beginning (but maybe it began even before) the tradition of Jewish intermarrying among themselves. This practice has led to the consequence that some rare metabolic diseases are found more commonly in Jewish descendants than other populations. Isaac is the only Patriarch who lived all his life in Canaan. Rebekah gave birth to twins 20 years after their wedding.

Jacob is the third and last of the Patriarchs. Esau (Jacob's twin) and Jacob may have been identical twins, as one was born 'red', and one 'white', possibly having twin-twin-transfusion syndrome. I've had them on my slides to describe this condition, in which, through a commonly-shared placenta, one donor fetus can give some of his blood to the recipient co-twin. Apparently Esau was born first, but Jacob bought his birthright from Esau 'for bread and a pottage of lentils' (Genesis, 25:34). Apparently Rebekah also favored Jacob.

Jacob married **Leah** (third Matriarch) and **Rachel** (fourth Matriarch). Seems a bit strange polygamy is part of this ancient history. Leah and Rachel were sisters. They were also daughters of Laban, son of Bethuel, brother of Rebekah (daughters of a first maternal cousin of Jacob). Jacob had six sons and one daughter from Leah, and two other children from Rachel (beloved wife). The last one of Rachel's children was named Benjamin, which means 'son', in particular 'last son'. Rachel died while giving birth to Benjamin. Isaac had also two other kids with Zilpah, handmaid to Leah. And two more with Bilhah, handmaid to Rachel. Total: twelve kids. From them, came the twelve original tribes of Israel. In fact, Jacob is also called Israel, after which the nation was named.

Around 1200 BC, **Moses** led the exodus of the Jewish people from Egypt. They reached the Holy Land, Israel. They settled in city-kingdoms, in the hills. At similar times, the Philistines, originating from the Aegean Sea, invaded and established 5 city-states on the coast. From their name, came the name Palestine.

Around 1000 BC, **David conquered Jerusalem**, united the Israelite tribes, and made Jerusalem the capital. King David is the first king of a united Israel. His son Salomon became king in 968 BC.

At gate A19, in Philadelphia International Airport, Paola notices about 20 men looking out the glass. Some hold their hands against the window, some hold their hands up, some hold books. Most have an undulating movement of their upper body, rocking forward and backward. Paola makes me notice them. They are praying. They must be looking east, towards their holiest place on earth. That is the Wailing Wall, or Western Wall. The only remain of their 2nd temple, destroyed by the Romans. We'll be there is 3 days. I can't wait. I bet they can't either.

Wednesday, November 24

On time, around 3:15pm local time, we land in Tel Aviv, at Ben Gurion airport. This airport is named after the famous general and first prime minister. Surprisingly for us, we encounter no problems at the airport, where passport control is very easy. In fact, security officers ask us usually more questions at US Customs when we come back from Italy, than here. We are ready for all kinds of questions. We have European (Italian) passports ready just in case the US ones cause suspicion. I have in my pocket the official program of the conference, and the emails of invitation. The lady at the Israeli Customs just takes our US passports and studies them for less than a minute, all 4. No questions. With a friendly smile, she sends us off. Very easy. So many prior fears were in vain. I let her stamp my passport, even if, some say, this might cause me trouble getting in or out of Muslim countries.

The trip has been organized in details. As soon as we pass Customs and get our luggage, we encounter a representative from the travel agency with the sign "Prof Berghella." She'll take us to the van.

But we have a great big unexpected surprise. Nachmy brings flowers for Paola, chocolates and drinks for the kids, a picture of me playing soccer for me. Nachmy is my good friend from soccer in Philadelphia. He is a super-nice guy, and having a friendly, well-known face greet us as we enter this new country, warms our souls. I'll never thank Nachmy enough of this unexpected, joyful reception. Even the travel agency people are impressed!

As I do in every trip, I have a wonderful discussion with the shuttle driver. He is the first true Israeli I can interact with in his own country.

While for Israel the capital is Jerusalem, for all other nations the capital of Israel is Tel Aviv. I'm very impressed as I begin to see the city coming from the East. It scrolls along the Mediterranean. Along the shore, the impression is that there must be almost as many skyscrapers as in New York City. And these are new, beautiful, shiny. It shows that the Gross Domestic Product of this new country has increased above 3% for the last few years despite the global recession. There is no sign of any financial crisis here. I'll see some poor, and very poor. But there are clearly some super-rich.

I begin to learn to pronounce some basic Hebrew words. 'Toda' is thank you. 'Bevakasha' is you're welcome, or please. The easiest and most familiar is 'shalom', used for both hello and goodbye, like the Italian 'ciao.'

The driver is very nice, and he tells us about Israel, the economy, the weather, a bit of politics. There is lots of traffic from Ben Gurion to the hotel. We are staying at the Leonardo City Tower Hotel, in Ramat Gan, a neighborhood of Tel Aviv.

We check in. The hotel is undergoing some repairs, but it is nice, modern, deserving of its 4-star status. I withdraw from the money machine some Israeli currency, called New Israel Shekel (NIS), or just shekel in common language. The guide had said $1 is worth 4 shekels, but it's already a bit less, more like 3.7 shekels. We walk around the hotel's neighborhood as we wait for the arrival of my sister's family.

Anna is married to Vittorio, and they are a wonderful couple. They have 3 great kids. Vincenzo, 19, is a new law student in Bologna; handsome, lady-killer, and extrovert, a lot of fun to be around. Margherita is 14, a freshman in high school, a poet, smart and past her tomboy stage. Livia is in her last year of middle school, is always well-dressed, loves to interact with adults, and is mature.

We meet Anna and the Masci's (Vittorio's last name) at the hotel. Our rooms are 1217-1218, their rooms 1205-1206, on the same floor. It's nice they came on the trip. The kids adore each other, and Vittorio and Anna have similar taste and interests as Paola and I, so we know we'll get along. They love traveling as much if not more than us.

It's late evening already, and we are jet-lagged. The plan is for dinner. We hail cabs on the corner, and negotiate the fare (as suggested in our guides). As we are 9, we need 3 cabs.

We have dinner at Abu Nasser on the hill. My colleague dr. Josh Copel had recommended it, as this is his favorite restaurant in the world (!). They serve us initially about 20 different small plates filled with different appetizers. The kids, to our surprise, try these different foods, especially Livia. I have a wonderful Saint Peter fish, apparently typical of the Mediterranean shore, which is right in front of the restaurant.

The restaurant is in Old Jaffa, maybe the oldest port in the world. We take great pictures as we walk around this old village.

Thursday, November 25

I go to breakfast at around 8am, as I have to be at the National Israeli Conference of Obstetrics and Gynecology at 8:30am. The 'spread' at the Leonardo Hotel is regal. Breakfasts in Israel are a real treat. They are buffet-style, and called *arukhat boker*. Small dishes, served cold, as an appetizer, are called *salatim*. The choices are endless, and all inviting. I try to be good, and have yogurt with delicious granola cereals, and orange juice. I do allow myself one chocolate croissant. I have time to say good morning to the other eight in the group, as they join me before 8:30am.

H-1 is the floor where the Israeli Ob-Gyn Society Annual meeting is being held. Everyone is rushing to check in. I mix in the large crowd, and find the vast convention hall. I even step to the podium, trying to put my slides in the computer. An attendant calls my attention, and invites me to his table. He quickly loads my slides. He'll be impressive in quickly bringing the slides up at exactly the right moments later on. I have 2 forty-five-minute talks on the program, plus questions.

I introduce myself to the secretaries at the check-in desk, and immediately they call dr. Jakob Bar. He's the President of the Israeli Ob-Gyn Society, and the person who officially invited me. He is very well behaved, sharp, good-looking, charming. He is very nice to me. He introduces me to at least 6-7 people. There crowd is >300 ob-gyns from all over Israel. They seat me at the main table, with the rest of the Board.

The whole program is in Hebrew, except my name, title, and talk subject. The program runs from about 9am to 2pm, with a small break. The first talk is on Israeli national statistics, and it is excellent. Unfortunately slides and talk are in Hebrew, but the head of the ob-gyn department in Jerusalem translates them for me. The numbers are great. Medicine and science in general are done at very high level here in Israel.

My talks go well. The subject is clinical, 'hot', controversial enough to generate lots of questions. The Israelis are not shy about asking difficult ones, or commenting they do not agree with what they heard from me. I defend myself as diplomatically as I can. I get lots of praise once back to the table from members of the Board.

Lunch is great, and the desserts are awesome. Kobi (as his close colleagues call Jakob Bar) explains to me that the food here must be kosher for people to attend. So the wonderful dessert with what I think is some kind of cream must not contain milk, as meat was served as well in the same buffet.

One of the many rules of kosher dietary law is that dairy products and meat cannot be mixed in the same meal. I wonder why this rule developed, possibly millennia ago. The rule to avoid pork is probably due to the fact that worms are often present inside pork, and surely caused disease in the past. Shellfish still makes us sick today if not properly handled, so it made sense centuries ago to stay away from it and its many dangerous bacteria. Another cogent kosher law for food preparation is to check the lungs for adhesions, which is a sign of tuberculosis. There are so many rules passed along to us by our ancestors. For some, it has made sense that they have stood the test of time, and of scientific verifications. Many others could be discarded given modern knowledge and current health practices.

I try to sneak out early, to be able to meet the other eight on the trip and go to the Museum of the Diaspora. It's the only Tel Aviv site mentioned in the book '1,000 things to do before you die.' I had planned to see it, and everyone else was kind enough to agree to the plan.

The Masci's, and Paola Andrea and Pietro, had spent the morning at the Tel Aviv shore, and then the kids demanded to enjoy the swimming pool of the Leonardo hotel. I find them in the hotel rooms, ready. We get in three cabs, but it's amazing this museum is almost not known at all by them. In fact our driver needs to ask several times for directions along the way. Anna and the kids' cabs drop them at the Hebrew University, far from the museum. I'm restless, as usual, and Andrea and I get in without waiting much, since it's 3pm and it closes at 4pm. Paola awaits the other six members of our family.

The museum is a bit disappointing, old, not very well organized, nothing that interesting. The movies are old, black and white, often hard to see.

Maybe the best part is the terrace of the bar. Except me, nobody else had eaten. So they devour sandwiches, drinks, coffee, etc. It's a beautiful evening, maybe 70 degrees, the sun sets slowly in the Middle East. We talk, laugh. Pietro Margherita and Livia ask permission and go roll down the grass slopes below. We find 3 cabs easily, and get back to the hotel.

Quickly we pick up sweaters, and we go to the Tel Aviv port area, on the beach. This neighborhood is beautiful, large, clean. The weather is again wonderfully warm, comfortable with just a shirt and no undershirt. We relax watching some young kids play beach soccer. They are super-talented, the ball never touches the sand. They hit it only with their bare feet, chest, or head. Even by Italian standards, they are very very good, the best I've ever seen!

Margherita Livia and I run to the shore, and touch the water: it's warm! It's dark out, and I'm fully dressed, so, surprisingly, the thought of diving in does not cross my mind. I must be getting old. Or just, finally, wise.

Paola and I take a cab back to the hotel, because at 7:40pm dr. Bar is picking us up for dinner. He drives us to a nice restaurant about 10 minutes away. We are about 15 around the table. The Israeli Ob-Gyn Society Board members, their significant others, Paola and me. I had asked for a typical Israeli restaurant, and I get my wish. About 10 different appetizers, all delicious. Plenty of hummus, tahini, etc. They brings us extra kebab with lamb, chicken, beef. A special liver dish, that I find tasty, tender, different.

The main dish is a fish for me that they recommend, and I see several others choose it, it must be good, I think.

The 2 male 'mfms' (maternal-fetal medicine specialists) in front of me are nice, affable, friendly, and I talk at length with them, but also with Kobi's wife sitting next to Paola, and Kobi, sitting next to me. He is very nice, and I may be too friendly, as I call him the 'president' often. I hope he took it well.

We have a wonderful evening. The desserts are again spectacular.

When we get back to the hotel, is about 10:45pm. Pietro runs and hugs us. He is crying a bit, scared that we were not back earlier. He soon calms down, and we go quickly to bed. Andrea with me, Pietro with mamma.

Friday, November 26

The breakfast at the Leonardo Hotel in Tel Aviv is again regal. The kids especially dive in the all-you-can-eat buffet. There must be 50 different foods to choose from, and they all look delicious. The kids have hot chocolates, croissants, fresh fruit, cereals, cheese and hams, omelettes, etc.

At 8am, we meet our guide, Aviram Politi. He says it's ok to call him 'Politi.' His Italian is pretty good. He has studied in Siena, and has Italian Jewish ancestors. He'll be a great guide, instructive, knowledgeable, courteous, flexible. Driven by Yuri, the Russian Israeli at the wheel, we are off to Jerusalem in our private minivan, just for us.

Jerusalem appears suddenly to my eyes. I had been concentrated on the history of this country, and the many anecdotes which Aviram had been telling us with the microphone while driving the scarce 1 hour of car trip between Tel Aviv and Jerusalem. Now 'White' Jerusalem is around the windows of our van. All the buildings here are made of the same beautiful local stone. Jerusalem is also called 'The city of Gold,' as this off-white, cream colored local stone is mandatory as a building material, and so the whole city is made of it, and its stone walls glow at sunset.

I love etymology, as it tells so much about the background of a place, or of anything. Jerusalem. The name comes from *Yireh* (an abiding place of the fear and the service of God), and *Shalom*, peace. We are in the most important city in our trip. We are in the heart of faith for billions of people, and certainly for us, since our births. I have imagined this moment, this opportunity, for a life time.

Streets appear clean, houses well kept. Some are elegant villas. Most Jews live here, outside the Old City, in West Jerusalem. Nothing is Arab-looking here. Later I'll see with my own eyes that instead most of East Jerusalem, including most of the Old City, are Arab in aspect and most inhabitants.

The city of Jerusalem is built on a series of hills, just like Rome. It has often been contested. Currently it's the capital of Israel for Israel, but not any other country in the world. It's divided mostly between Jewish and Muslim quarters. On the Middle East map, it's at the border with the West Bank, mostly populated by Muslim Arabs. But its history is so complex that only a graph (below) can make things a bit clear for the foreign interested in possibly the most contested territory in the history of our world.

Overview of Jerusalem's historical periods (Source: Wikipedia)

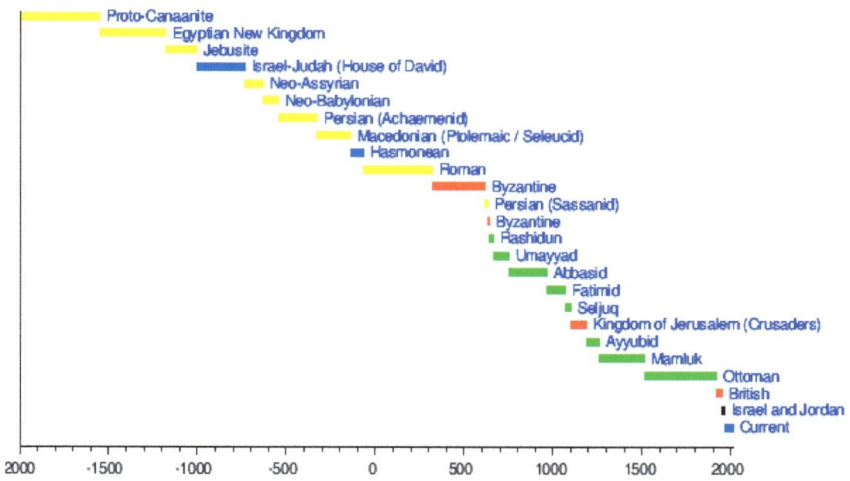

Yellow: ancient kingdom, pagan (multitheistic, several Gods worshipped)

Blue: Jewish rule

Red: Christian rule

Green: Muslim rule

As can be seen, the city changed from multitheistic to Jewish to Christian to Muslim to Christian to Jewish rule back and forth over the last 4 millennia. Anyone can stake a claim on these hills based on history. Only one people have the best-selling book in the world to support their claim.

Our van arrives at our hotel. The Inbal Hotel, at 23 King David Street, is a 5-star hotel, beautiful, modern. I'm a bit ashamed we can all afford it. Well, the truth is, both the Leonardo and the Inbal, for the full 4 days total, are compliments of the Israeli Ob-Gyn Society, and I'm grateful and honored, as well as a bit proud. Our stop is only about 10-15 minutes. The time necessary to unload and store our luggage at the hotel, and visit the clean and elegant bathrooms.

The Old city is what really matters to all in Jerusalem. It's what hundreds of thousands, may be million of people have died for over the millennia. It is still divided, but messily, in 4 quarters: Muslim, Christian, Jewish, Armenian. There are about 35,000 inhabitants living here, sharing this holiest of Holy Lands with millions of tourists every year.

To save time, Yuri drives us the 5 minutes towards Mount Zion, leaving us at the Zion Gate, one of the entrances to the Old City. Just in front of this gate, there are two 'holy' places, one on top of the other, so important to the history of the world, which I had highlighted on my guides and in my brain.

One of the first 'holy' sites that we visit is the **room of the last supper**, or **Coenaculum**, or Cenacle. It's a grey room, bare of any furniture. There is not even a table! It's a 14th-century 2nd floor room, and there has been so much construction upon construction here that is not even clear what building this room belongs to. Mark 14:15 does refer to a 'upper room' for this historic event. "…a large upper room furnished and ready". The room is not particularly large, and is not furnished.

One thing is clear: what for Christians is the Last Supper, was for Jesus and his 12 disciples a Passover dinner. Mark 14 does indeed say that this is where "[Jesus] I shall eat the Passover dinner with my disciples." So many overlaps between Judaism and Christianity. This is also the room where Jesus' disciples, gathered on Pentecost 7 weeks after his death, were filled with the Holy Spirit and began to speak foreign languages.

There is nothing to recall these events. In fact, there is an Arabic inscription in the Gothic windows, and another window is blocked by a *mihrab*, an alcove indicating the direction of the Mecca, much like in a mosque. Interestingly, one floor below, is one of the most important Jewish sites.

The **Tomb of David** may not have been here, as this was not where Jerusalem really was in the 10th century BC, but a 'new' tradition now 1,000 years old wants the tomb of the first king of the united Israel here.

Aviram Politi, our guide, instructs us to divide. The women go to the left. The men must come with him to the right. Like at the Western Wall, like in any synagogue, like in any religious Jewish place, men and women cannot be close to each other. Paola, Anna, Margherita and Livia are a bit at a loss, but they go to the left, by themselves, without our guide.

Why is this? Who first came up with this rule? I think of the Christian 'gineceo,' the upper deck of ancient churches were the women worshipped, while only males were allowed in the main elected floor of the church. Why? Yes, the Bible, in its 10 commandments, says to not desire someone else's woman. And I do agree that 'not to see is not to think about.' But often we fantasize on what we do not see, on what's missing.

On the right, on the 'male' path to the Tomb of David, we see right away some Jewish head covers, called in Hebrew 'kippas', made with thin cardboard. We have to wear them to get into this Jewish holy site.

The tomb is large, covered by a purple velvet cloth. The cloth is inscribed in golden Hebrew symbols and texts. I think of Napoleon's tomb, again much larger than his tiny occupant. King David, who lived about 3,000 years ago, must not have been huge. Certainly, the size of its tomb is more appropriate to the consequences of his life for humanity, than the size of his body. Andrea, Pietro, Vincenzo, Vittorio and I pray with our kippa-covered heads down, in this tiny room in front of the massive purple-covered casket.

The Old City of Jerusalem is still encircled by the 500-years old Ottoman-Empire-built walls, and can be entered only by gates in the walls. We get in from the Dung Gate, after walking along its outside perimeter for 200-300 meters. They are majestic.

The whole of Jerusalem is saturated with prayers and dreams, with religion, with worshipping, with people praying everywhere. The various religions seem to want to outdo each other in terms of who prays more, who has the best-looking places of worship.

The **Western wall** is Judaism's number #1 religious site. This is what St. Peter's in Rome is to Christians, and what Mecca is to Muslims. To understand the history of the 2 Jewish temples of Jerusalem is to understand Judaism itself.

The first temple was built by **Salomon, son of King David**, around 950 BC. The temple becomes the religious center of Judaism.

In fact the terms Israel and Judah come from the two regions in which the kingdom split at Solomon's death in 928 BC. The **kingdom of Israel** was the northern kingdom. The **kingdom of Judah** was the southern kingdom. After initial conflict, these two kingdoms lived alongside each other peacefully. In 721 BC, the *Assyrians* conquered the kingdom of Israel, taking its residents eastward to captivity. This is where the 'ten lost tribes' myth starts.

In 586 BC, the *Babylonians* defeated the Assyrians. The kingdom of Judah is also conquered by the Babylonians. Their king Nebuchadnezzar destroyed Jerusalem and the first temple. Jewish survivors are exiled to the 'rivers of Babylon'. This is the first 'Diaspora', the dispersion of Jewish people throughout the world. This historic event, which might seem foreign to most non-Jewish readers, is in fact famous in most cultures. For example, the famed Opera by Giuseppe Verdi called 'Nabucco' retells this exact story. There is an aria, 'Va pensiero' ('Go my thoughts') which has signified and continues to signify the yearning for freedom for all oppressed populations. When Verdi wrote it, Italians sang 'Va pensiero' yearning for freedom from foreign control.

In 538 BC, only 50 year later, Cyrus the Great of *Persia* (currently approximately Iran) conquered Babylonia, and permitted the exiles to return to Judah. Jerusalem is rebuilt, and the <u>second temple erected</u>. Persian Empire rule ended in 333 BC, when *Alexander the Great* defeated them.

In **63 BC, the Roman Empire** conquers Judah and these Middle East regions. In 66 AD, the Jews rebelled. The Romans fiercely defeated the revolt, and <u>destroyed Jerusalem and the second temple</u>. The Western wall is what remains of the west part of this second temple. In fact, it is not even a part of the temple itself, but a part of the defending wall around the temple. The exact location of this temple, in the vicinity of today's Dome of the Rock, is now lost. The Western Wall is called also Wailing Wall, because of the Jews who pray and cry in front of it. Another big Diaspora starts. 'The Wall' (*Kotel* in Hebrew) is there to remind Jews all over the world of these hardships, for the last 2,000 years.

Being a Jewish religious site, men pray on one side (left), women on the other (right), without any possibility of mixing or even seeing each other. This Wall is like a synagogue, and in fact more than one, for rabbinic Orthodox authorities. There is even a check point to see what's inside our bags, but it is quite loose, gentle, almost friendly.

There are probably a few dozens Jewish men praying on our side. They are wearing proper attire for their prayers. They, as well as Andrea, Pietro, and me, wear the kippa, the circular head cover.

Why the kippa? The *Talmud* states "Cover your head in order that the fear of heaven may be upon you." The Talmud is a central text of Judaism, as it records originally oral rabbinic discussions pertaining to Jewish law, ethics, philosophy, customs and history. The *Mishneh Torah,* compiled between 1170 and 1180 by Maimonides, a prominent Egyptian Rabbi, dictates that a man is required to cover his head during prayer. It makes sense for them and us to be wearing it now.

Andrea, Pietro and I, wear the obligatory white kippas happily. We take a free space in the Wailing Wall. It is a massive wall, built with huge 'Jerusalem' rocks, the white rock, which glistens in the sun. We put our open palms against the Wall, at shoulder height, and lean towards it. I start a prayer, spontaneously. In Italian. "Dear God, thank you for all you have given us. We are so lucky to have been given so much love. Such a wonderful family. Please bring peace to the world.'

It had been Daoud, my long-time cherished Algerian Muslim friend who had advised me to pray here for peace in the world. It seemed to me that the best place on earth to pray for peace in the world is right here in Jerusalem. My impression is that many, if not most wars, are started for religious reasons. While we pray touching this sacred wall, we can hear Islamic prayers coming from above, from the Temple Mount where the Muslin Dome of the Rock is. And earlier we had also heard bells ringing, from a nearby Christian Church.

As I finish my brief prayer, I tell God that now Andrea wants to say a few words. To my surprise, his voice is trembling a bit, as he has been crying. He is really moved. He must have understood, even at 12 years of age, the importance of this holy place. He also thanks God for his great family, and his happiness. He 'passes' the prayer to Pietro, who also says some words of gratitude, in serenity and inner joy.

Happy and moved, we now place our previously prepared piece of paper in the wall. The prayer I'd written in it: "Pace nel mondo," Peace in the world. Andrea and Pietro study for 3-4 minutes the cracks in the wall, to select a good one. The first 2 or 3 they try are inadequate, as the piece of paper, crumbled up, does not stay 'in' the wall. Finally, they spot a tiny hole, where the piece of paper with Peace in it fits and 'sticks' well in the Wall.

Interestingly, the cracks are cleared of the millions of pieces of papers with prayers inside them several times a year, and never simply dumped. They get eventually buried in sacks in a Jewish cemetery, as they often contain God's name.

The **history of religion** has fascinated me ever since I was a child. **Judaism** is the oldest of the current most popular monotheisms. Abraham, the first Patriarch, broke from the pagan pluri-deistic Babylon, and made a one-God new creed. He lived around 1,800 BC. 3760 BC is when the world started according to Jewish creed, and in fact for Jews we are currently (2010) in 5770. Judaism is at least 4,000 year old, may be more. **Christianity** was founded by a Jew who lived in Palestine, now Israel. While Jesus is recognized as a prophet by Jews, he was God reincarnated for Christians. While Jews still await a Messiah, we have had ours, and are waiting for a come-back. Jesus was born probably around 4 BC in Bethlehem, now a Muslim town. And he died in Jerusalem, now in Israel, around 29 AD. Most of his teachings happened between 26-29 AD, around the Sea of Galilee.

Christianity is about 2,000 year old. It can be regarded as a 'rib' of Judaism, and the 2 religions are certainly close cousins. Actually, as Pope John Paul II rightly said, Judaism is father to Christianity. We share the same exact Bible, the same commandments. Jesus' last supper was a Passover meal.

The differences, especially between Judaism and Christianity, are not huge. The similarities are much more profound. The **Torah** is the Jewish book of the 5 first chapters of the Bible. It is also called the 5 books of Moses. In the Bible, it is called the Pentateuch, and it consists of Genesis, Exodus, Leviticus, Numbers, and Deuteronomy.

Christianity is currently the religion with the most followers, about 2 billions.

Islam is a 3rd relative, somewhat more distant. Muslims are more than a billion and a half (about 1,600,000,000), 23% of the world's population, and 63% are in Asia (2009 Pew census data).

The Jews are only about 15 millions (15,000,000), a rough estimate. 5-6 millions live now in Israel. About 6 millions are in the USA. The rest, all over the world. Over half of the world population holds Jerusalem as the holy ground of its religion. No wonder fighting for supremacy has been going on here for so many millennia. But we humans like to emphasize the differences in general, in any human relationship, and forget the 99.9% (including of DNA) that makes us exactly the same.

Interestingly, in Israel there is no civil marriage, only religious marriage. Both partners must be, or convert, to the Jewish faith. Otherwise, they must marry abroad.

The Wailing Wall gets even more venerated around **Jewish holidays**. What are the major ones?

Shabat occurs every week, from sundown Friday to sundown Saturday
There is no driving, cooking, traveling, answering the phone, using money or doing business, writing, etc.

Passover is the celebration of the exodus from Egypt, lead by Moses. It is a 7-day holiday, with the 1st and last day as most religious, and dietary restrictions. Instead of leven bread, *matzo* (unleven bread) is used. The first night the events of the exodus are recalled, and a high symbolic meal called the *seder* (Hebrew for 'order') is eaten together. It occurred March 30, 2010, and its date changes every year.

Rosh Hashanah is the Jewish New Year. It begins a 10-day period of introspection and repentance. Jews attend long synagogue services, with apple and honey to hope for sweetness in the New Year. It occurred September 19, 2010, and its date changes every year.

Yom Kippur is the most solemn day of the Jewish year. It is the last of the 10-days following Rosh Hashanah. These 10-days are the High Holy Days. Much of Israel comes to a halt, with roads completely empty. At night fall, the holiday ends, and people can break the fast. September 28, 2010, changes every year.

Hannukkah is a non-religious holiday. A Jewish rebellion in the 2nd century BC regained control of Jerusalem. The Temple was regained, and in it a vessel was found with enough oil to burn for a day. Miraculously, it burned for 8 days. From this event, this holiday now lights 1 candle a day for 8 days. The candelabrum is called *hannukkiah*, and usually has a 9th middle candle which is lighted the first day with a 2nd (1st) light.

We walk all around the area. On the left side of the Wailing Wall, so on the men's side, towards north, there is a recently dug tunnel, which shows a long strip of this wall, with some of the huge stones weighting 400 to 570 tons. One can see how many different remnants of ancient constructions exist on this part of the world, inhabited for at least 5,000 years. Jerusalem is indeed a layer-cake of time. Each period built over the other. Each new religion, or return of power of one, laid new buildings on top of the ones of the defeated.

From the Wailing Wall, Aviram Politi takes us towards the Christian sites. It's interesting we actually go mostly through the Muslim quarter. The atmosphere is that of the *souk*, or Arab bazaar, everywhere. In fact, most of the Via Dolorosa (Stations of the Cross) is populated now by Muslims shacks, little shops, etc.

As a Catholic, I grew up knowing these stations as the Via Crucis, from Latin. Here most refer to it as the Via Dolorosa, which is clearly in Italian. It is also called the Way of Suffering, or the Way of the Cross, or just The Way, in the universal current language, English. It is the route that Jesus walked, carrying the cross. It goes from the place of his trial, to the site of his crucifixion and burial. There are 14 'stations' or stops of the Cross. Some are scriptural, such as I, II, V, VIII, and X to XVI. Some are not, such as III, IV, VI, VII and IX.

I do notice, as we are walking in a Kasbah, full of Muslim, lead by Aviram, a sign saying Station III. I ask Aviram if we can follow the Via Dolorosa, if possible from the beginning. I would have imaged a site full of Christian Crosses, and Catholic sculptures and paintings, but the small streets are mostly Arab-looking. There are not too many Christian pilgrims that I notice. We go up a small road, on a 10% or so incline, towards Station I. The street looks like one of the ones in Erice, or of many other medieval small towns in Italy. On the side of the street, there is a small shop which sells Turkish coffee, pomegranate juice, and other Arab drinks and food.

Station I is where Jesus was tried and condemned by Pontius Pilate. There is very little left of what I would image was there in 29 AD. On the left side, Aviram points to the top of a wall, perhaps where Pontius Pilate would have stood.

Station II is where Jesus was scourged and given the Cross. We do notice in the street, now going back downhill, that there is an entrance, labeled Ecce Homo Covent of the Sisters of Zion. Ecce Homo, or 'This is man', and I remember this phrase to underline the suffering of Jesus, made a poor, hurt, destitute man, like the ones who suffer the most on our planet. We arrive at a crossroad, with Wad Road, one of the Old City most important streets. To the right, the street climbs toward Damascus Gate. To the left, we would go back to where we came from, which was the heart of the Muslim Quarter, back towards the Western Wall. Here everything feels Arab.

Station III is where Jesus falls for the first time. It is near the crossroad between Via Dolorosa and El-Wad Road. Across the street, on El-Wad Road, an Arab bazaar is the main attraction. Almost hidden, on our left, is the chapel, built by Free Polish Forces after World War II, which commemorates this station. Nothing grandiose, as none of the stations are. We turn on El-Wad Road to continue to the next station.

Station IV is where Mary embraces Jesus. This is a few steps beyond Station III, and the south corner where El-Wad Road meets a new stretch of Via Dolorosa. I think of all the churches, everywhere in the world, where these 14 Stations are represented and worshiped. I think of the artists who, over 2 millennia, have been commemorating and reliving these 14 stations with sculptures, with paintings, with roman numerals and Christian votives. Apparently, the tradition to replicate these stations within churches comes from St. Francis. When the Franciscans took control of Jerusalem in 1372, a Via Sacra was developed also in Jerusalem. It was not until 1731 that Pope Clement XII extended the right of all churches to have the stations, provided that a Franciscan father erected them, with the consent of the local bishop. At the same time the number of the Stations, which previously varied between 10 and 30 or so, was fixed at 14.

Station V is where Simon of Cyrene picks up the Cross. It's at the same corner, near Station IV. From here, the Via Dolorosa turns right, and begins its ascent towards the Calvary.

Station VI is where a woman wipes the face of Jesus. Her name is Veronica, from *vera* (true in Latin) and *icon* (image in Greek). In fact the image of Jesus' face remains on the cloth. I think of all the several churches in the world which claim to have some piece from this Via Crucis. The Sacra Sindome, in Turin, supposedly is the cloth where Jesus was laid on after coming down from the cross. A little piece of wood from the Cross, in several churches around the world, including my native Italian region, Abruzzo. Station VI is about halfway up the street of this stretch of Via Dolorosa, marked by a brown wooden door. At the top of the street, on the corner of Via Dolorosa and Suq Khan-ez-Zeit, is Station VII.

Station VII is where Jesus falls for the second time. The first fall was at station III. It's interesting these episodes are not reported in the Gospels. They might be my favorite stations. They depict the difficulty of Jesus in carrying such a heavy burden. The weight of our sins. And they also remind me of the difficulties encountered by each of us in every day life. These stations bring me visions of us humans falling at times, overwhelmed by disease, poverty, lack of food or drink, lack of love and affection. These are the things that make religion close to the people. Where each of us can find a piece of himself, see himself in Jesus, and embrace these creeds, for better or for worse.

In Jerusalem, for Station VII, there is a chapel, containing one of the columns of the Byzantine Cardo, the main street of the 6th-century Jerusalem. Station VII is on the busy Suq Khan e-Zeit: what a name for such an important Christian site.

Station VIII is where Jesus addresses the women in the crowd. It is marked only by an inscribed stone in the wall on the left.

Station IX is where Jesus falls for the third time. Here there is just a column as a marker. We actually miss it. Via Dolorosa is not straight. It is in fact at times a zig zag. Station IX, as station VIII, is off this path, and we do not see it. Probably Aviram figures there is not much there to see. It's the last of the stations not mentioned in the Gospels. I think that the Via Dolorosa is pretty long. And we even skipped some of its length. It would have felt much, much longer with a cross on top of one's shoulders. And it is almost never flat, it goes down and then up, up again and then down, just like life.

We arrive in a small square, irregular, coming down a few steps. Aviram tells us that in front of us and this court is the Church of the Holy Sepulcher. Stations X through XIV, or 5 of the 14 stations, are inside the Church of the Holy Sepulcher. This is the site of the death, burial, and resurrection of Jesus. In a way, it is unfortunate there is so much construction here. I would have imagined just a hill, a cross, and a cave. Two millennia of construction over these holy sites now make them unrecognizable.

The church is outside the city walls of the time of Jesus, since no executions or burials took place inside the Jerusalem city walls in Jesus' times. The first church here was built in 326 AD by Helena, the mother of the emperor Constantine the Great. He was the emperor who made Christianity the official religion of the Roman Empire. The one we have in front of our eyes is the fourth church built on this site. It was built in the 12th century by the Crusaders. But the inside has been refurbished several times, including an almost complete rebuilt after a fire in 1808.

Station X is where Jesus is stripped of his garments. It is supposed to be on the Golgotha, the Calvary, meaning 'the place of the skull'. Indeed we have to take very narrow stairs on the right of the church. They are small. I think I would have never found them without Aviram.

Station XI is where Jesus is nailed to the cross. A wall mosaic at the front of this chapel on the upper level in fact depicts Jesus being nailed on the cross. I do not notice it, or at least forget I've seen it. Later, while I read the description and history of this church outside, in the courtyard, I state I did not see it. Pietro says that indeed it was there, he saw it. I'm glad he did, and proud of his observational skills, and attention.

Station XII is where Jesus dies on the cross. This is the most important site, I think. And it is completely Greek Orthodox-looking. The central chapel is all candlelight, oil lamps, and Greek Orthodox icons. Luckily, while most people gather here, clearly making the place which gathers most attention, it's not crowded. I see a lady bent under the small golden altar, inside the front columns which sustain it. She is kneeling down, and leaning towards the back of the altar, on the floor. As she gets up, I cannot resist the curiosity to check what she was looking at, and doing. There, completely away from the casual visitor's sight, is a silver disc, with a hole in it. Inside the hole, supposedly stood the cross where Jesus was buried. I put my hand over this hole and pray, as I saw the lady do before me. I do think that it's a bit strange to have such a holy place so hidden and tough to appreciate. I'm the only one of our group to do so.

It's really hard to imagine that here stood the Golgotha of biblical memory. There is no hill. There is only a 2-meter-square piece of rock on the side of this station XII. It's impossible to appreciate if this is really native rock, attached to earth, or just a piece brought here at some time to remind us of the Golgotha. There is no soil. And... how could the cross, which is not here and is only represented by an almost invisible hole, stand on rock? Many doubts remain to the tourist, even a well-read one.

I think of all the Good Fridays, and sometimes Fridays during Lent, in which Christian worshippers relive the Via Crucis, in millions of representations and events throughout the world, every year. I think of the many sculptures and paintings of Jesus on the cross I've seen in my lifetime. For example, the beautiful one in the church where I used to sing in the choir as a 'chierichetto', an altar boy, la chiesa Sacro Cuore in Pescara. The ground is a rocky hill, with a green field around it. Here at the actual site of the crucifixion of Jesus Christ, there is nothing even remotely reminiscent of any of the paintings I've ever seen.

Station XIII is where Jesus is taken down from the cross. There is a bust of Mary in a cabinet to the left of Station XI commemorating this site. This does look like a Catholic Madonna, may be the only place in the Church of the Holy Sepulcher which reminds me of the hundreds and hundreds of Catholic Churches, paintings, and sculptures I've seen in Italy, Europe and 3 other continents. So station XIII, 'geographically', is really before station XII. Confusing.

Station XIV, the last one, is where Jesus is buried. To reach it, one has to go back to the main floor, downstairs from where we are. Aviram says we are lucky, because the line is only about 15 minutes-long, instead of the usual 2-hour. This site is given a privileged position. It's in a chapel in the middle of the main part of the Church of the Holy Sepulcher. The line moves quicker than I expect. The guard manning it is austere, and reprimands often unruly tourists. One enters a tiny door, only about a meter tall. I have to bend in 2 to sneak through it. The tiny room inside the chapel where Jesus body would have been laid is disappointing. It's tiny, I could not fit horizontally in it, and it's barely as tall as me. There is an altar, and a marble ledge where the body, supposedly, would have been laid. I fit inside with Margherita, Pietro, and Livia, I think. Nobody else would fit in this tiny, miniscule, place. And it's claustrophobic. I pray aloud with the kids a 'Padre Nostro', and by the time we are at 'Dacci oggi il nostro pane quotidiano', the guard is already yelling we must get out to let the next tourists in. Not exactly a mystic experience. The massive Wailing Wall inspires crying, not this tiny room.

As said above, Stations III, IV, VI, VII, and IX are not specifically attested to in the gospels. In particular, no evidence exists of station VI ever being known before medieval times.

Station XIII, representing Jesus' body being taken down off the cross and laid in the arms of his mother Mary, seems to embellish the gospels' record, which states that Joseph of Arimathea took Jesus down from the cross and buried him. Some Christians would like to add other stations, especially one depicting the resurrection of Jesus.

To provide a version of this devotion more closely aligned with the biblical accounts, Pope John Paul II introduced a new form of devotion on Good Friday 1991. It's called the Scriptural Way of the Cross, has also 14 stations, but they all represent episodes mentioned in the gospels. I'm not aware that centuries of tradition and thousands of Via Crucis in thousands of churches around the world have been replaced by these new 14 stations, approved by Pope Benedict XVI in 2007.

Inside the Church of the Holy Sepulcher, we have a few more minutes to explore some other sites. Plenty of legends live inside it. The impression, as in so many sites in Jerusalem, is that there has been construction upon construction upon construction, and much of what was original is gone, or mixed and adjacent to something completely different. Aviram takes us to a large chamber where there is a little place called 'the center of the world.' Paola states that Foligno (a small town in Umbria) is the center of the world according to the people there, as it is near the geographical center of Italy. Pietro remembers, from our trip to Macchu Picchu, that Cuzco was the center of the world for the Incas, and its name means 'umbilicus', to testify its centrality. I think then that all humans want to be the center of the world, and this has not changed through time and is similar throughout the world.

Despite my studying before getting here to this church, what I was not ready for was the fact that it is shared by so many Christian denominations. Clearly, the dominant one is the Greek Orthodox, allowed to be so by the Ottoman Empire which dominated these lands for centuries. It was Russia who pressured the Ottoman Empire to give so much dominance inside this site to

Russian-style Greek Orthodox icons, paintings, candles, rituals, etc.

There are at least 6 Christian denominations which divide control of the Church of the Holy Sepulcher (la Chiesa del Santo Sepolcro, in Italian). These are: Greek Orthodox, Latin (as Roman Catholics are known here in the Holy Land), Armenian, Egyptian Copt, Syrian Orthodox, and Ethiopian. Often they fought for control of different parts of this church, sometimes violently. The current divisions are the result of the 1852 Status Quo Agreement.

Thinking back, I'm not surprised now that Christianity, in particular Catholicism, does not have here its main Holy Site. Saint Peter in Rome, where nothing as 'holy' has happened, is the center of Christianity. But here in Jerusalem, these sites so wonderfully depicted in the Gospels, and so vivid in the imagination of about 2 billion Christians, fail to make someone feel this is truly a holy site. First, the environment outside in the street is Muslim. Second, inside the church, nothing of the gospels is recognizable. The different factions of the Christian faith divide each little space, and fail to give it a warm, holy feel. There is no soul to it. The Western Wall, bare but massive, never changed, symbolizing the suffering of its faithful, and is magic in its holiness for all Jews. The Temple Mount is powerful, large, soaring against the sky, sumptuous and elegant in its large square for all Muslims. Nothing similar can be said of the Church of the Holy Sepulcher, which is dark, inhomogeneous, at times cold and impersonal, too Russian Orthodox in general (at least for my Western European background), with few, too few true remnants of the site it wants to celebrate but has cancelled from our eyesight.

We continue to walk among the Arab bazaars. One gallery leads to the Temple Mound. We actually arrive near it as hundreds of Muslims are coming down from their prayers. Unfortunately, we cannot climb the stairs and visit the Temple Mount, with its famous Dome of the Rock. This area is restricted, and only Muslims can access it at this time of day.

Sorina Grisalu is the head of the department of Ob-gyn in Jerusalem, and we had become friends the day before in Tel Aviv. Sitting next to each other at the Board-member table during the conference, she had kindly translated the lectures in Hebrew. To my surprise, she had volunteered to help us while in Jerusalem. When I told her that we had a guide all day, she proposed we'd go out to dinner together. I did try to say 'No, thanks, do not worry', as we just met and I did not want to abuse this new acquaintance. But she insisted, and said she'd call me at 6-6:30pm the next evening, i.e. tonight to check if we could/would.

Punctual, she called, and really gave me no choice: "I'll come and pick you up at the hotel around 6:30pm, and then we'll go to dinner at the YMCA near the hotel." I'm surprised she's willing to go out on a Friday night, since this is the start of the shabat, when Jewish people are supposed to observe the religious, biblical rest. But Sorina Grisalu had said she was not 'that religious', not orthodox. So she shows up on time at the Inbal with Ricardo and Ben.

Ricardo is her nice, polite, handsome, tall, Argentinean-Jewish husband. Ben is her last son, named Ben therefore appropriately. We walk all as a big family up the road to the YMCA. This is an elegant restaurant, and we get seated outside. Before appetizers, Sorina points to the ceiling, where there are still bullet-holes in the cement from the 1967 war. It's an anticlimactic moment, as the evening is warm, pleasant, and very calm, due to the shabat. One cannot imagine the fury of war in such a classic, elegant, distinguished setting.

Sorina is a volcano of information. She is seated near Anna and Vittorio, and they hit it off grandiosely. She gives us great information regarding Israel and her hometown Jerusalem all night. Her parents background is Romanian. She speaks many languages, and understands some Italian. She is a quintessential Jewish woman. Determined, smart, hard working, bright. She says herself that her husband calls her 'crazy', as, despite 3 kids, she works 10-12 hours a day, comes home after 9pm, with her neurologist-husband left to make dinner and tend to the house needs. Clearly she is a river of activity, and cannot be contained. She loves to be busy, helping women give birth to healthy kids.

Through Sorina, I understand once again how the more similar one is, the higher is the chance to fight. In fact, perhaps Sorina's most disliked people are Orthodox Jews. They are called Haredim (in Hebrew). Secular Jews like Sorina do not get along too well with them. These are the ones who wear black hats, black clothes, the yippa all the times. They accept word-by-word all of the 613 commandments of the Torah. They strictly follow kosher eating rules. They have their own political party, and much political weight in Israel, at least according to Sorina.

We spend a wonderful evening with Sorina and her husband Ricardo. They are candid and insightful in their opinions, and are extremely knowledgeable about Israel and its people. It's funny how complete strangers can exchange so much revealing information. For me, it's a window to a fascinating world I did not know about as much as I wanted.

The Inbal Hotel had left in our room Executive Suite passes, compliments of the Conference I was invited to. Paola is busy, so I invite my sister Anna, who I know loves this stuff. We toast to a great trip, and indeed great lives, with white wine which she finds in the living-room-like Suite. It's a wonderful life.

Saturday, November 27

We leave at 8am for the Dead Sea. First, Yuri our driver, and Aviram our guide, take us to the Garden of Olives, on the hill on the Eastern side of Jerusalem. From here, one can enjoy great views in early morning of Jerusalem. You cannot imagine the many battles this city has witnessed looking at the peaceful view of Jerusalem from here. From here, one can even see our hotel Inbal, shaped a bit like a pleated skirt, imposing, also made of Jerusalem rock but definitively modern and massive.

To head towards the East and the Dead Sea, we pass a 'check point'. Given the fact we are in mostly desert land, and everything around looks pretty peaceful, the check points seem an unnecessary exaggeration. But our guide reminds us that in 2001 and 2002 thousands of civilians were killed from Arab suicide bombers, and since then these checkpoints seem to have been associated with a decrease in these events.

The second and major next stop is Masada, the palace-fortress on top of a plateau overlooking the Dead Sea. King Herod was a brilliant builder and paranoid leader who reigned over Israel as king of the Jews by the grace of the Roman Empire in the 1st century BC. Herod had redeveloped this 18-acre site on top of cliffs 1,400 feet high over the desert. This was one of his many palaces, a possible refuge from his many external and internal enemies. Herod died in 4 BC, with the palace still doing well.

The Romans had destroyed the second temple in 66 AD, and, by 70 AD, had destroyed Jerusalem and crushed the Jewish revolt there. Some of the Jewish people had still tried to resist them. Around 72 AD, a few of them, the last to defy the Romans, retreated to Masada, one of King Herod's palaces, on the western side of the southern-central part of the Dead Sea.

The Roman general and governor, Flavius Silva, was determined to end the rebellion, and so built 8 legionnaire camps around the fortress on the plateau. For at least 1 year, 960 Israeli men, women, and children resisted. The Romans catapulted small soccer ball-size rocks to the top of the mountain, some of them burning. But even though several died, Masada's brave still refused to give in to surrender and captivity.

So the Romans built an assault ramp on the Western side of the mountain. It is still visible. History shows that Masada was at last conquered by the Romans.

The historian Flavius Josephus wrote the last hours of the Masada resistance, as told to him by survivors. No proof exists of this story, which is one of the most famous in Jewish history.

The night before the Romans were to go on the final attack, the rebel Jewish leader Elazar Ben-Yair gave a rallying speech. He convinced the less than 100 still alive to 'neither serve the Romans nor any other save God.' As they had no hope to resist the Romans and sure captivity, they committed mass suicide. The guide shows us ten pieces of rock with Hebrew names written on it. On each one of them is the name of one of the last 10 rebels drawn by destiny to kill the rest of the residents. The story says that then 1 was drawn to kill the other 9, and then commit suicide.

When the Romans walked in, they found about 92 bodies. One hidden woman with a child lived to tell this macabre story, according to our guide. So Masada is where the Jews held on to the Romans up to around 73 AD. And most Jews are extremely proud of this story. These heroes at Masada chose death to captivity.

This is one of the most famous heroic stories of Judaism. Sorina, the night before, had told us she did not like this story at all. Israelis chant the valor of suicide, a better option than slavery under Rome. She said they should have surrendered. Staying alive gives more hope than giving it all up with suicide. It's so interesting to see history from the perspective of a native like Sorina. Nonetheless, Masada is impressive, built many centuries ago, and you can feel and imagine its tragic resistance.

During Roman rule, in 132 AD, another Jewish revolt, led by Bar-Kochba, broke out. In return, Emperor Hadrian leveled Jerusalem in 135 AD, and changed the name of this now Roman region to Syria Palestina. Most of the remaining Jews left this part of the world, not to return for almost 2 millennia.

In about **325 AD, Emperor Constantine made Christianity the official religion of the Roman Empire. A few years later, unfortunately, he made it the only allowed religion**.

On the way towards the Dead Sea, I see a sign for Ein-Gedi, a famous kibbutzim, and ask to stop there. I had seen it listed in one of my favorite travel guides, '1,000 places to see before you die'. It's supposed to be one of the most beautiful places in Israel. Aviram and Yuri were nice enough, at the last moment, as we were driving by it, to steer off the road and climb towards it. We have been driving for miles with a uniform landscape of burnt brown and beige desert rock. At the entrance, I wonder why this place makes it in the '1,000 places' book. The middle-aged, well-mannered Israeli who collects the 90 shekels from me for the entrance fees states that they live through tourism here, not really any more as a commune kibbutzim.

As we start the path along this somewhat mysterious place, we are all surprised at the lushness of this oasis. Very interesting, from here you can guess the history of how the Israeli got beautiful oases from the desert. This is a luxurious green garden. The baobabs are impressive.

We stop at an Ahava shop, where Paola, but especially my sister Anna, buy many spa-like creams, shampoos, wrinkle-preventing Dead Sea products to maintain their beauty. They are so excited. I spend the time perusing the small mostly grocery shop on the other side, where I buy 2 wonderful books, titled 'Understanding the Old Testament,' and 'Understanding the New Testament.' I'm very happy with them, I love history books, and these are simple and clear.

Then we go on to a resort hotel on the Dead Sea.

The Dead Sea should absolutely be one of the geographic 7 wonders of the world. Like the Grand Canyon in the US, it is indescribable to the ones who have not been there. The Dead Sea is in the lowest point of dry land on earth, at 1,373 feet below sea level. 410 meters below the level of the sea.

It is a big lake. I've seen pictures in many books. As we drive on its western coast, at times one cannot see the shore on the other side. By then one can, and realizes that Jordan is visible, near in some points, almost a swim away.

The 'Sea' is made by water containing an astonishing 32% salt. This water is 9 times saltier than the ocean! This is because water flows here from the Jordan river and other sources, but has no way of flowing out. Evaporation, in this desert land where it is often sunny and very hot, leaves a massive amount of salt behind.

The buffet lunch is luxurious. The fish is moist, tender, delicious. Then to the beach. We change at the SPA, getting towels. This next event is one of the most memorable experiences of the trip.

We had brought our swimming suits from over 9,000 kilometers away just for this. The weather is beautiful, 80+ degrees Fahrenheit, perfect for the 'beach'. The lush resort has a swimming pool, and a Jacuzzi, which I'm sure are comfortable and luxurious, but I encourage everyone to head for the shore.

The 'sea' water is super clean. No sign of pollution. No sign of any waves. There is barely any breeze, but it's not too hot. The Dead Sea appears clear, calm, 'dead,' in front of us. There are no waves hitting the shore, which looks a sandy-looking light cream color.

Vincenzo, Livia, Andrea are already in. They are cheerful in delight. They seem to float on the water. The key to 'handle' a bath in the Dead Sea is careful movement. One must lean little by little on one's back, and float. Swimming, if necessary, must be done slowly, by rotating backwards one's arms. It's paramount not to splash, and to keep the head well above water. Margherita splashes her face a little with Dead Sea water, accidentally, and for a while we fear for her eyesight as she screams in agony from the severe burning.

Andrea, who has a miniscule scratch on his skin, says it is burning. Vincenzo, and later each of us, complain that our anus is also burning from the super-salty water.

There are many more amazing things here. Floating upright, one's body is pushed so high that nipples show. What looked initially like sand, is really salt. Where one cannot touch with his feet the bottom, there are salt crystals as big as tennis balls. With some effort, we manage to 'fish' out with our feet a few of these 'balls.' They are fragile, and most break on our touch. The few we retrieve are made of sparkling white salt crystals. Amazing. If one licks his finger wet with Dead Sea water, the strong taste is bitter, stingy.

The Dead Sea is in great peril. The guide had told us that the water level was 25 meters higher just a few years ago. In fact, I had read that the water level has been receding about 1 meter a year due to the lack of rainfall in Israel's north (feeding the Jordan river) and, of course, human activity. Israel, Jordan and Syria all divert water away from the Jordan River for drinking and irrigation. Less than 7% of the river original water flow reaches the Dead Sea.

While I watch Yuri drive, and I hear again his heavy accent, I remember of the over 1 million Russian Jews which are now Israelis. They are the biggest ethnic group. They have their own, conservative, party. You can tell from his interactions with 'Vladimirs' and 'Borises' we cross during the trip that they feel in charge, that they are a powerful group, feared by others, such as our Italian-ancestry Jewish guide Aviram Politi.

Sunday, November 28

We had previously missed to go 'on top of Jerusalem,' which to me and I think most objective observers is the flat rectangular piece of land on the eastern side of the Old City of Jerusalem. Here there is now the Temple Mound. It is full of mosques. The enormous plaza contains also *Al-Aqua* mosque, which represents the Islamic 3rd most important holy site, after Mecca and Medina.

Islam is the most recent of the 3 monotheisms which fought over Jerusalem. They are the last to claim it as their 'Holy Land'. In fact, Mecca and Medina are more 'holy' for Islam. But Jerusalem, while never mentioned in the Koran, is important for them, too.

Muhammad's *hejira* (flight) from Mecca to Medina occurred in **622 AD**, marking this date as the beginning of Islam. This religion is therefore about 1,400 years old. About 600 less than Christianity, over 2,000 less than Judaism. For Muslims, 622 is the first year of their calendar. Muhammad died in 632 AD. His followers burst out of Arabia, a bit like the Christian apostles did out of Israel, and spread his word. This was also an actual empire, based on the new creed. The Muslim empire would at some point extend from Spain to India.

The Temple Mount is the top of Mt. Moriah, one of the highest grounds in Jerusalem. Therefore close to God, and most valued by all religions.

The Jewish tradition identifies this as the site where Abraham erected an altar and prepared to sacrifice his own, only son, Isaac. This is for Judaism the foundation stone of the world. Jewish tradition also states that here King David made a repentance offering to the Lord (II Samuel 22). And where his son Solomon built 'God's House', the so-called First Temple. So it was here that the 'First' and 'Second' Jewish temples stood for a total of about 1,000 years. In fact, to expand the Second Temple on a grand scale, it was King Herod who leveled off the top of Mt. Moriah with thousands of tons of rubble. The massive retaining walls include some of the largest building stones known, each many hundreds of tons. He created this flat, rectangular, 'shoe-box'-shaped, huge space on top of Jerusalem. But the Second Temple was reduced to smoldering ruins by the Romans in 70 AD.

Even Christians have some tradition on this most-contested of religious sites. In the New Testament, Jesus disputed points of law with other Jewish teachers, and overturned the tables of money changers. He also predicted the destruction of the Temple, while looking down at it from the Mt. of Olives. Interestingly, the Templars took their name from this very place, where they set up their headquarters. Some believe the Byzantines may have somewhat ignored this place, believing it was cursed.

In this same site, Muslim point to the imprint of a foot, regarded as that of Mohammad himself. It is here that tradition wants Mohammad ascended to heaven for his meeting with God. This is called Muhammad's 'night ride'. Awaken by the archangel Gabriel (who by the way is important for Jews, Christians, and even Muslims), he is taken by the winged horse *el-Burak* to *masjid al-aqsa*. So this is 'the farthermost place' named in the Koran. Muhammad met then God face-to-face, and received the teaching of Islam. From heaven, he returned to Mecca the same night.

Muslims call this area *Haram esh-Sharif*, the Noble sanctuary. Interestingly, Jerusalem is never named in the Koran, so the identification of the 'ascent' of Muhammad with the Mt. Moriah is attributed to later Muslim tradition. Our Jewish guide says it was guided by politics. By the wish of the new religion to take over and destroy the old religion and its sacred site.

In 638 AD, the Arab Caliph *Omar Ibn-Kahtib* conquered Jerusalem from the Byzantines. To celebrate the ascent of Muhammad to God, the Dome of the Rock was built in 691 on the Temple Mount by Caliph *Abd el-Malik*. This is certainly the most prominent building in Jerusalem, the most easily recognizable from the distance, the one in the cover of every tourist guide to Jerusalem. It is a shrine, not really a true mosque. *Al-Aqsa* is a true mosque. Interestingly, in the 12th century, it was the headquarters of the Templars.

One can only compare the beautiful calm of this bright, sunny Sunday morning to the fury of the past. I imagine some of the conflicts going on this hill for centuries, millennia really. In fact, in 1951, King Abdullah I of Jordan was assassinated here inside *Al-Aqsa* mosque. Peril could occur any time. I'm not surprised. While geographic and architectural beauty is all around us, I predict that something hugely violent will happen here this century. It's an easy prediction given the past and current circumstances.

We wonder around. The flat Temple Mount is huge, 35 acres, or 11 football fields. Some of the buildings are architecturally clearly not-Muslims, and in fact the mosque in front looks like an old Romanic traditional church, like so many of 12th or 13th century churches seen in Europe.

I try to enter the Dome of the Rock. The guard initially looks at me friendly. He asks me where we are from. I say 'Italy'. I think he was expecting I were from a North-African or Middle Eastern country. Then, with a hopeful look, he asks me if I'm Muslim. I have to answer the truth: I am not. He seems disappointed and startled that I'm not Muslim. His face soon turns stern, and he walks a couple of steps towards me, ordering me away from near the entrance. I cannot get in.

Why can't we enter, peacefully and respectfully, this mosque? Why can't we even walk around this large square, so beautiful? Historically, this has been a sacred place for other religions, too. Why such fanaticism? Clearly the attitude one feels is that Islam is the best, only true religion, and only Muslims can spend time on this, the best site in Jerusalem. Not fair. At 10am, we are 'forced' out. We had been able, just like ALL others, to enter the Holy Sepulcher. To pray at the Western Wall. I do not get the double standard.

Around 1pm, Anna and the Masci's leave us to go to the airport and back to Italy. We had a great time together. So Paola,

Andrea Pietro and I decide to go to the Mount of Olives. The view is magnificent, and we take quite a few pictures. This is where Jesus taught, and wept over the city (Luke, 19:41). This episode is commemorated by the tear-shaped Dominus Flevit ('The Lord weeps', in Latin) church, a bit down from where we take pictures.

There is a walk down from the Mount of Olives, also known as the Palm Sunday road. It is just wide enough for one car. Most traffic is by Christian faithfuls on foot. Sometime a taxi goes by, trying to entice some of us to jump in. This road leads to the ancient olive trees of the garden of Getsemani. This is where Jesus was kissed by Judah, and then arrested.

The garden is small compared to what I imagined. But there are still beautiful, ancient olive trees, perhaps 20-30 of them, close together, just as I would see them in a farm in my native Abruzzo, in the Center-East part of Italy. Their trunks are very wide and, Andrea says, 'old looking.' In fact, some of these olives are said to be the same ones Jesus saw, and touched. They are over 2,000 years old. The curving and twisting of these trees reminds me of the pains Jesus went through around the time of his betrayal and death.

Adjacent to this garden, is 'The church of all the nations.' It has a brilliantly colored mosaic façade easily seen from many parts of Jerusalem. It looks, and is, somewhat modern, built in 1924. In front of the altar, there is the Rock of Agony, where Jesus is said to have endured his Passion. In fact, the older name for this church, more appropriately, was the Basilica of the Agony.

Recommended in my Fodor's guide, I want to get us to the Garden Tomb, where some say is the real place of the Calvary and then burial of Jesus. Once we get there, by a longer-than-expected taxi ride, it's closed. While disappointed, I realize that research says this is probably not the true burial site of Jesus. I'm less disappointed as a scientist, more as a tourist.

We are in a completely Muslim quarter, and it's a bit scary with the kids and no cab in sight. We soon realize, Paola and I, by looking at a map, that the Damascus Gate is close. So we walk there, perhaps 200 meters.

Jerusalem had been under Muslim rule for over 400 years when the Popes decided it was time the 'wrong was righted', and the Holy Land returned under Christian rule, as it had been under the Roman Empire. From this thought, came the **Crusades**. Again, a war due to religion. The Crusades are just another stupid loss of thousands of lives due to religious creeds.

In **1099, the Crusaders conquered Jerusalem**, and massacred Muslims and Jews. So many stories and historic figures from these historic events have been told to us in school, or even in fables. Saladin was a Muslim king who resisted the Christian invaders. Richard the Lionheart, or King Richard I of England, was one of the most famous Crusaders.

The **Muslims conquered again Jerusalem in 1265**, with the Mamlucks. Outstanding Muslims architectonic sites in Temple Mount (*Hara mesh-Sharif*) and all over Jerusalem were built.

In **1516, the Ottoman Empire**, ruled by Turks, defeats the Mamlucks and takes control of Jerusalem and Syria. The walls around the Old City of Jerusalem were indeed built by the Ottomans. Politi, our guide, who is Jewish, states this fact like it's something minor. The walls look beautiful to me, even if it is one of the newest things in Jerusalem, only 500 years old. Around the walls, there are several entrances. One of them is the beautiful Damascus gate.

There are several cabs there around the Damascus gate. We take one to the City of David, where we want to go to Hezekias' tunnel. This is a tunnel from the times of Herod. When Jerusalem, his new capital, was about to be attacked by the Assyrians, the Jews in Jerusalem realized they would have been soon left with no water. So they ingeniously dug channels down deep in the rock below the city walls to connect the water running just outside the city walls on the Kedron Valley to the city. Some began digging from the Valley, knee deep in the water of the underground streams, and some began to dig from Jerusalem. Miraculously, not only they dug quickly, but well enough, since they connected! Imagine the happiness when water began to flow, deep underground and hidden, from outside to within the city, being able to save the population of Jerusalem from sure draught. The tunnel is named after King Hezekiah, the king at the time.

Andrea wanted to go through the whole tiny tunnel, which goes thigh-deep in water for 45 minutes. In one of my few moments of sanity, I say 'no', agreeing with Paola. We 'settle' for walking in another tunnel, barely 6 feet 4 inches tall (just enough for me), and less than a yard wide, claustrophobic but doable. More importantly, dry now, without any water.

I had emailed Nachmy, who agreed to come visit us in Jerusalem. We meet just outside the City of David, near Dung Gate. He is with his father.

Clearly Nachmy is a Jew. A modern, enlightened, to my eyes tolerant Jew. He is a lawyer, met an American Jewish girl when she came to Israel, married her and moved to Philadelphia 9 years ago. He is one of the best soccer players I've ever met. And I've met many, including Brazilians. I'm delighted to see him.

But how did the Jews get back in these lands, when their rule was ended in 66 AD by the Romans?

Interestingly, **around the 1880's, only about 50,000 Jews lived in the whole of the Palestine region**. This was mostly a desert, a region ruled by the Ottoman Empire, and where Arab nomad Bedouins did not use the land much for agriculture.

Zionism is the world for the wish of the Jews to get back to what they feel is their land. As stated also in the Bible, the book most sold and read in the history of the world. The first World Zionist Conference was organized by **Theodor Herzl** and took place in 1897.

Tel Aviv was founded in 1909. Degania, the first kibbutz, was established the same year in the southern shore of the Sea of Galilee.

World War I, among many other changes, caused the end of the Ottoman Empire (which had sided with Germany and lost).

Britain, victorious, took control of the region of Israel, while France took control of Lebanon and neighboring countries. Also in 1917, the British government expressed some support for the creation of a Jewish homeland in the Balfour declaration. Tensions between Arabs and Jews began.

A British Commission in 1937 recommended partition of the land into 2 states. In 1939, a 'White Paper' is issued by Britain restricting Jewish immigration to Palestine, and forbidding Jewish purchase of land.

During World War II, in the meantime, the Nazi's kill 6 million Jews, an amazing two-thirds of European Jewry, in the Holocaust.

In **1947**, in a truly historic vote, the United Nations vote for the formation of a Jewish State in Palestine. Lebanon to the north, Syria and Jordan to the East, and Egypt to the south are all Arab states surrounding this new nation.

In **May 1948**, **David Ben-Gurion** declares Israel an independent Jewish state. He is Israel's general and first Prime Minister. Eretz Israel, the land of Israel. **600,000 Jews** now lived in their own state. Immediately seven Arabs countries invade the new state. Israel survives the invasion. For many reasons. For Jews, by miracle. Certainly, because when you defend from 'invaders' what you think is your land, God-given land, you are tough to defeat. For others, because of thousands and thousands of good arms sent in by the USA, in particular, together with lots of money and supports from wealthy Jews worldwide. And, probably, also because of limited coordination of the Arab armies, which acted somewhat disjointly from each other, and certainly outnumbered the enemy.

A cease-fire agreement is signed in January, 1949. Transjordan (now Jordan) annexed the West Bank (also called Cisjordan) and East Jerusalem. The regions around the holy River Jordan have always been particularly fought for. Egypt annexed the Gaza strip. Even now, Gaza is controlled by Arabs, and Cisjordan is populated mostly by Arabs. It is here that Jewish settlers continue to build houses, despite a UN mandate not to. But by building settlements (mostly kibbutzim) all over Palestine in the 20th century, the Jews were able to convince the world that this is their territory. Their will has been extraordinary.

Palestinian Arabs living in the new Jewish state mostly fled or were expelled. So a new Diaspora started, this time of Arabs instead of Jews. Some Arabs stayed and became citizens. Even now, in 2010, Arab Muslims represent about 25% of the population of Israel, and number over one million. In Jerusalem itself, proclaimed the capital by the state of Israel, there are 400,000 Jews, and also 300,000 Arabs.

In 1949, the new Israeli state passes the Law of Return, allowing any Jew to get citizenship just based on religion. Massive immigration soon followed. Interesting, almost a million Sephardic Jews from Marocco (in particular), Algeria, Libya, Egypt, and other north African countries, and from Syria, Lebanon, Iran, Iraq (in particular), the famous Yemenite communities, and other Middle Eastern nations immigrated to Israel between the 1940's and 1960'. Israel's Jewish population doubled within 3 ½ years, and tripled within 10.

In the 1990's, after the end of the cold war in 1989, massive Russian Jews immigration began, over 700,000 moving from the former Soviet Union. **Ashkenazi Jews**, the Jews from Europe, mostly Eastern Europe such as Russia and Poland, dominate Israel and its politics today. **Sephardic Jews**, who came to Israel from Arab lands, including Spain, are under-privileged.

The Palestine Liberation Organization (PLO) was founded in 1964. They refused to recognize Israel, and wanted an independent state for 'Palestinians'. Israel's independence is to Arabs the *Nacba*, the 'Catastrophe.'

In 1967, in the 'Six-Day' War, Israel occupied East Jerusalem, Gaza, Cisjordania, and the Golan heights.

In 1973, a coalition of Arab states attacked Israel on Yom Kippur.

In 1982, the Lebanon war was an Israeli invasion and occupation of Southern Lebanon.

In 1987, the *intifada* (uprising) brought sustained Palestinian Arab unrest.

In 1994, the Oslo Accords were signed, mutually recognizing Israel, the PLO, and Palestinian autonomy in the Gaza Strip.

In 1999, after Ehud Barak was elected Prime Minister, Israel withdrew from southern Lebanon.

In 2001-2002, the second *intifada*: suicide Arab bombers terrorized Jerusalem and other Israeli cities, with terrorist attacks targeting especially populated public places as markets and buses. Jerusalem was like a ghost town, according to Sorina. By the end of this second intifada, in 2005, 3,000 Jews and Arabs were dead.

In 2005, Israeli occupation of Gaza ends, so that this territory is now under autonomous rule. In 2006, Hamas won elections in Gaza unexpectedly (at least for those living outside this part of the world).

Currently, there are about 1.5million Palestinian Arabs living in Gaza. In the West Bank, under Israeli rule but partly autonomous, 2.4million Palestinian Arabs share this land with less than 200,000 Israelis. It's here that we hear the controversy of new Jewish settlements which are not authorized by the United Nations.

In the rest of Israel, there are about 7 million people. Over 75%, almost 6 millions, are Jewish. Of these, at least 15% are orthodox, and follow the Torah (the 5 books of Moses, or the first 5 of the Bible) literally. They do nothing on the Shabat (from Friday dusk to Saturday dusk), and keep kosher. The Haredim, or ultra-orthodox, wear black hats and suits. Their wives cover knees and elbows, and often wear wigs to cover their hair.

Over 1 million are Muslims, of which about 100,000 are still Bedouins. The Arabs are mostly mainstream Sunnis. There are about 100,000 Druze, Arab-speaking and followers of a separate religion which broke from Islam around 1,000 AD. There are only about 100,000 Christian Arabs.

The Muslims do not serve in the military, so to avoid Arab versus Arab fighting. The Druze do serve.

It's fitting that we are going to leave Israel from Ben Gurion, the airport named for the 'father' of the new state of Israel.

We take the 11:55pm flight back, Tel Aviv direct to Philadelphia. After less than 30min in the flight, they call for a doctor. One man just in front of me gets up, and so I sit down again. After about 4 hours into the flight, in which we mostly sleep soundly, they call for the same doctor again, to go back to row 2 for help. Soon after, while I try to sleep with Andrea lying on my shoulder, I begin to feel the plane going down. I realize, while my eyes are still closed, that we are probably going to make an emergency landing somewhere, given the medical situation.

Monday, November 29

In fact, 15 minutes after I begin to feel the plane going down, the captain does announce what I had feared. We will be landing in Frankford, Germany, in 15 minutes, due to the medical emergency. My watch is already set at Philadelphia time, and it's about 10:30pm in Philadelphia now. We land at about 4:30am Frankford time on Monday. The plane stops in the middle of the runway. I see a fire truck outside. The airplane doors open. They tell us all to stay in our seats, as paramedics rush in.

They wear bright red overalls. I see them now up in business class. They are attending someone who must be lying on the ground. One is doing chest compressions. She is busy 'pumping' the chest, doing CPR. I hope, for the man especially, CPR quickly works, and they can take him to a more proper place for more medical attention. But CPR continues, for over 30min. We find out the doctor in front of me is an anesthesiologist. He soon confirms what I fear. The man has died.

Still, the paramedics do not leave. 5:30am. I begin to fear they must be doing lots of complex paperwork. And they must be thinking about getting a new crew, new pilots and personnel. I fall asleep again. After 6am, the pilot does confirm: our flight is now cancelled. We need to get off the plane, check luggage, and find ourselves some way back to Philadelphia.

I realize I may not make my meetings, my in-house call shift. Well, given the death on the plane, one must put things in prospective, and I take it in stride, without getting too upset. Paola Andrea and Pietro are wonderful, not complaining.

The fight to get a seat on the USAir non-stop Frankford-Philadelphia flight is fierce, as hundreds of people want it, with the German authorities initially not prepared to host and accommodate us.

We go to Starbucks, and get plenty of sweets and caffeine. Later, we see a nice black man, looking out the window. He asks us if what he sees outside is snow. He says he is from Barbados, and has never seen snow. He must be at least 35! Andrea and Pietro are surprised. Yes, it is! Oh my, we may get delayed because of snow, now.

Luckily, I am a Platinum member of US Airways, Paola a Gold member. We eventually board the Frankford-Philadelphia flight. It's snowing outside. We sit over 5 hours on the plane, while Andrea and Pietro play cards the whole time, waiting to get de-iced. No such luck. Around 6pm German time, they tell us to get off the plane. It'll be until after 7pm before we get our luggage back, again. At 9pm we finally get to a hotel and some food. There are at least 20cm (8 inches) of snow in Frankford. In the meanwhile, by phone, I have us booked for the Frankford-Philadelphia flight leaving on Tuesday at 12:45pm. We have to expect a 'deja-vu' day tomorrow.

Tuesday, November 30

Tuesday we do take the flight back to Philadelphia. A Jewish woman sits next to me, smart, pretty, petite, talkative. She works for the NIH, another accomplished, bright and driven member of this religion. We are exhausted, and all I want is some quiet, but especially to get home. Which we finally do accomplish. Even with a 36-hour delay, and plenty of misfortune, all these minor bumps on the road (at least for us) have certainly been worth a fabled trip, the trip of a lifetime.

Front cover

Wishful pieces of paper in the Western Wall, Jerusalem

Acknowledgments

Andrea P. Berghella, Amen Ness

www.ingramcontent.com/pod-product-compliance
Lightning Source LLC
Chambersburg PA
CBHW040355190426
43201CB00037B/13